SEASONED EYES
ARE BEAMING

Jovannah Bär

I0521772

SEASONED EYES ARE BEAMING
Jovannah Bär

Published by CBS Green Man Publications, in May 2018,
on behalf of Invisible Voices of Brighton & Hove,
as part of the Invisible Voices programme
for the 2018 BRIGHTON FRINGE FESTIVAL.

ISBN: 97890 82783 629
(NUR CODE 373)

Author: Jovannah Bär

Cover image by Jack Savage, photographer and digital artist
http://www.jacksavage.co.uk/
https://www.facebook.com/jacksavagephotographer/

Author photograph by Craig Neesam

Interior artwork courtesy of The Graphics Fairy
https://thegraphicsfairy.com/free-victorian-frame-clip-art/

I'd like to dedicate this book to:

Nils, for giving me the confidence to write,

and Tamar, for helping me to get to know myself, and introducing me to the safest conditions I've ever known,

and Jack, for providing an inspiring cover image.

CONTENTS

Part Three: On a Lighter Note

Part Four: For the Record

Part Five: What I wanted to Say Was

Foreword

Writing this bundle has felt like an absolute freedom. Thank you so much for buying my work, my carefully written words.

It has been an absolute pleasure to take part in this project. Invisible Voices is an incredible platform to give invisible people in our society a voice. This year we are supporting Cascade Recovery Café, First Base, and Sussex Homeless Support. These are all causes built by incredible, driven people, who are willing to exchange their time and energy to give help to those who need it and come to seek it.

I believe giving help is sometimes just as brave as asking for it. So many people are not in the place they deserve to be. It's not just about being a human being taking part in society, it's about standing up for the basic life standards I believe you're entitled to as a human. I believe everybody is entitled to a safe environment to call home, and to feel safe amongst a group of people that will provide you with unconditional support. Unfortunately, this is not always the case. There are people incredibly hungry, lonely and endangered as I write. Hopefully, my words will make a small contribution for those in need.

The concept of aging has always intrigued me. At only twenty-one years old, I often laugh about the things I did or the way I thought when I was younger (some of the things are not as funny as I wish they were). You know, I can only imagine how I will eventually laugh about the events and feelings that are hard on me today. I wish I could have a sneak peek at the knowledge I have not yet earnt. Unfortunately, the time machine has not been invented yet and I will just have to improvise, like I've always done.

All the love,

Jovannah

Part One: Observations

Once

Most of the streets out here

Were built for a specific reason.

Some are very quiet,

Next they're crowded for a season.

Like the ones that will bring you,

From the city to the sea,

Full of expensive sport cars

Driving fast, unconsciously.

Probably not even noticing,

All the work that was put in.

Once this freeway was a sketch,

All that's made,

Once had to begin,

With the scratch of a pencil.

Indescribable Beauty

Have you ever had a close look

At those colourful butterfly wings?

It's like a piece of art in the museum

You may admire, but not touch

A single item in the collection of things.

Nature is like a gallery

For the most special, wonderful looks.

People have grown to want to define them,

But some things are just so wondrous

They cannot be captured in books.

To Govern

Sounds were being absorbed

By the clouds which were patiently waiting

To join the newborns on their journey

As the politicians were debating,

Nearly fighting over the budgets.

Could money not better be spent,

On pursuing the war in some faraway country,

To raise the status of their own land?

While the real images were being repressed,

From the conscience of the decision-maker.

Making it harder and harder

To reign in compassion,

Since the academic is never

A convicted law-breaker.

I heard the whispers saying they'll take over

The minds of the opportunistic youth.

And I'm starting to see this power trip,

Based on a series of twisted truths.

While there is a long line of children,

Looking for a sound place to sleep.

Why is the strength of our combined forces,

After centuries still falling into the deep?

Do they really see sense in this strategy?

I will not ever forget the sound

Of a tortured scream.

Why are those who are supposed to protect us,

Treating history like some long lost dream?

All I Know

I should not be
Too stubborn.
Oh, and one plus one
Is two.

A square won't
Fit into a circle,
But head plus heart,
I should combine these two?

(Human) Being

The first thing I remember,

Is how it simply felt to "be".

This was before there was thought,

I did not hear, nor did I see.

'Being' was nothing but the knowledge,

Of my existence, I was there.

This was before I made connections,

I did not love, nor did I share.

I think I wasn't even breathing,

Felt like my soul was out to roam.

Just floating there between the lights,

Until it attached itself to a home.

The Piano Man

He likes his things to be perfectly normal,

He prefers the days to be ordinary, all the same.

He needs his usual spot in some quiet corner,

He won't play,

If he thinks he can't predict the game.

For some unknown, kind of mean reason,

I seem to enjoy catching this man off guard.

I guess it was the unplanned, shaky moments,

That gave him the opportunity to show his heart.

I have never been a woman to simply love,

And am certainly not a person to blindly hate.

I know just how to express

Every bit of kindness in me,

But I'm in the wrong

When I keep showing up too late.

The piano man loves the instrument

For its predictability,

When it's alright, it makes this sound

So very involuntarily.

It's not alive, it has no will,

Still, it's got some magic beans to spill.

So I keep smiling as if it's permanent,

I will not fall out of my role,

Music makes us feel so safe,

I've always considered it beautiful.

Talk of War

While life had turned quite peaceful,
The streets were tensed in an everlasting hurry.
The eyes of the crowd always looking up,
Scared, wondering, in worry.

I had never known what war was,
I had only heard, I had only read.
But I sensed that so many people knew,
A malicious monster I had never met.

Where are we supposed to go?
There's no hiding from death above.
Hold on, don't lose, don't break,
Just eat, play and love.

I kept thinking of possible reasons,
To award so many innocents with pain.
Has not every human that's touched the earth,
Sought shelter from the same drops of rain?

I can't bear it, I can't see it,

I don't know why one is better than the other,

A boy is always someone's son,

That woman might be somebody's mother.

Where are we supposed to go?

There's no hiding from bombs above.

Hold on, don't lose, don't break,

Just eat, play and love.

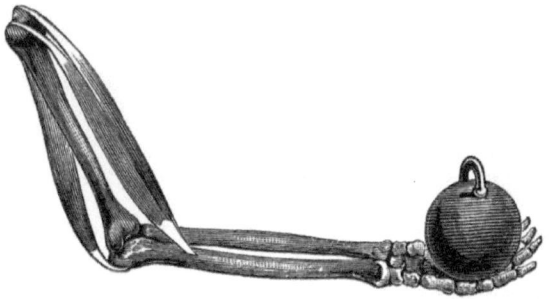

Carried by Green Arms

"Being small is not that bad."

I thought to myself, whilst climbing a tree.

Up here, carried by green arms

There's a world grown-ups can't see.

I once asked my father to climb up too,

He tried, but never quite made it to the top.

He said that if he'd dare look down,

His poor old heart would stop.

From then on

I knew that climbing,

Was a treasure, meant just for me.

Up here, carried by green arms,

I am mighty, I am free.

We Are Deadly

By domesticating animals
As much as we possibly could,
We are no longer seeing the world,
In the way we really should.
A place for numerous beings,
To live, to eat, and to sleep.
Life, for all on the planet,
To enjoy, to grow, and to keep.

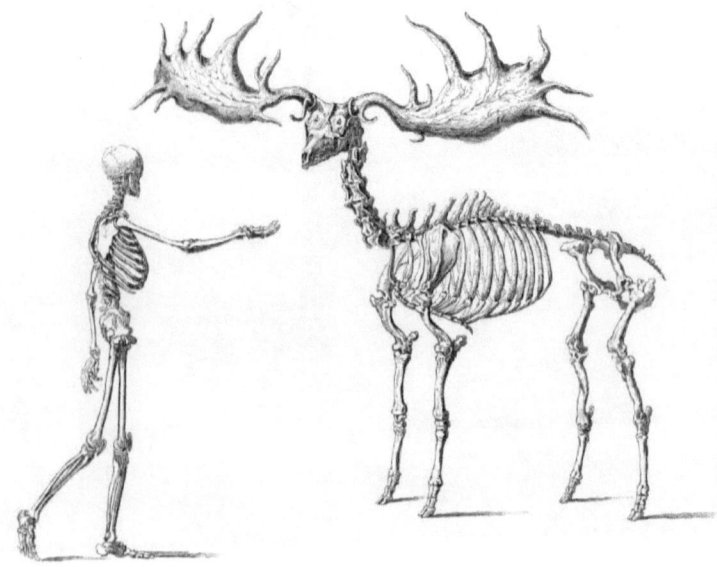

My Hands (Part 1)

Woke up very tired

As if my battery's unwired

As if nothing I would eat

Would give the energy I need

Half my sleep is interrupted

Half the leaders are corrupted

And I'm watching all this happening,

>With the ropes,

>All out of my hands.

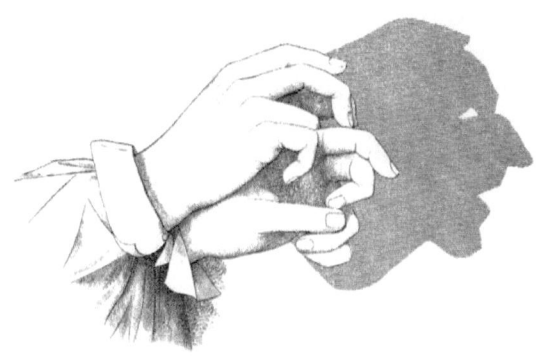

Part Two: To My Recollections

To Undress the Knight

The inside of my head is filled

With clouds, instead of brains.

Confusion is running through my veins,

I am so tired.

These dreams are more vivid than ever before

I cannot reassure myself anymore.

Is it my wrong, do you condemn me

For the crazy way I'm wired?

And so I'm counting the dots on your dress,

For a moment I feel a little bit less,

Please, don't look at me,

Let me be part of the background.

Don't you let me unfold,

I'll lose grip of the shield that I hold.

And there's no time in your schedule,

To pick up my pieces off the ground.

I don't know how much of me you can take,

Don't want you to think I was born a mistake.

Is something terrible happening when

I lose it, and end up crying again?

And so I spend every minute around you,

Hiding what's happening, the things that I do.

For I would rather pretend to be okay,

Than to risk driving you away.

My Hands (Part 2)

I am angry cause I'm small

Most of people look so tall.

I am angry for the marks,

On my legs, my back, my face.

I am furious for the words,

And the way abandonment hurts.

I am angry 'cause I'm angry

And there's no one to scream at.

                    Went to work so very tired

                    As if my battery's unwired

                    As if my fingertips still bleed

                    Give me the stitches I so need.

                    Half my night is cut to pieces

                    Oh the fear, it never eases

                    And I'm feeling all this happening,

With the ties

Around my hands.

Secrets

The sound of silence

May be quiet,

But the longer I listen

The more I hear.

The deepest sense

Of discord

Is an insatiable black hole,

Hungry for my fear.

The sound of silence

May be quiet,

But it turns deafening

Over time.

I believe it's always

The silence that covers

The most horrific,

Unforgivable crime.

Playing Dead

It's raining as the sun goes down,
The leaves are on the ground.
The wind is blowing joy away,
The birds don't make a sound.

I'm lying here all by myself,
I'm now the perfect prey,
The animals are getting close,
Claws and teeth not far away.

They'll take me to a darker place,
Or is it a different light?
Should I wait to see what comes,
Or get up and face the fight?

It's raining as the sun goes down,
I am silent as I wait.
The wind is blowing joy away,
Who cares? It's far too late.

To have A Voice

I'm trying to stay positive,

By taking life just as it is.

But I must always remember,

To never settle for this.

All this prescribed gratitude,

Has never saved my day.

Not once did someone ask me,

If I had something to say.

Anatomy of Love

There might be a hundred kinds of love,

And it's more than just an emotion.

I can't define it, though I've tried.

Love is so very painful when it's not replied.

Love can be a teacher,

Love may push you off-track.

Love is unconditional,

You cannot turn and take it back.

There might be a hundred kinds of love,

And it's more than just a state of being.

I can't explain it, though I've tried,

Love isn't over, once somebody has died.

Love can be a motive,

Love can be a shield.

Love is a two-edged weapon,

The scar remains a weak spot,

Even when the wound has healed.

To me, love mostly travels one way,

I open my heart, but then they'll run away.

While my love is very loyal,

It's made me very strong.

Even in times of unreasonable hate.

Love's watched over me all along,

The loveless road I've travelled,

It's taught me to truly see,

If I want to be loved by someone,

Love has to begin with me.

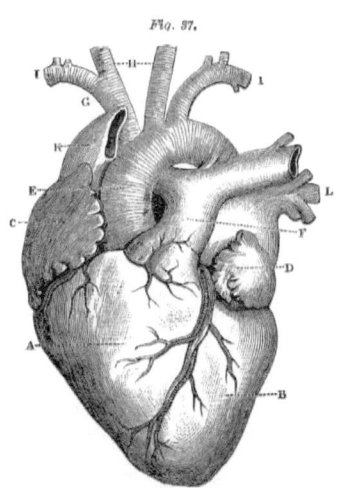

Fig. 37.

Lullaby

Word for word
I can remember
The song you sang
To me.

And when I sing
Into my head
There's a picture
I still see.

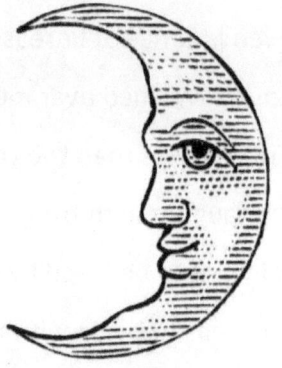

But I can't bring
The sound back
And I have lost
Your face.

In my past you're
Still so present
How could you
Ever be replaced?

Trauma

No pause, no night, no defeat,

No fall, no break, no bleed,

Could have ever prepared me.

                              The silence surrounds me.

A coincidence? A trap? A rescue?

The smell of the monster, that screams at you,

Nothing else has ever scared me.

                              The silence astounds me.

The shock, I'm blown, I'm numb,

The silence after the bomb.

His heated eyes still stare at me.

One of Three

My name is Zoe,

I was defined from the start.

Born as one of triplets,

I have always been a part.

A part of their selection,

We must always be the same.

And if I'm a little slower,

I am quick to feel ashamed.

My name is Zoe,

And I am now 15 years old.

I looked a little chubbier,

Than my sister, I was told.

Pound after pound,

I starved them all away.

Still no one ever told me,

When I was doing okay.

I have been in the hospital,

For 3 years now, alone.

Wondering why people,

Still don't see me,

As my own.

We Lost our Future

When I was six my dad took me to a house,

The last one he would – in his life – call home.

When we left this place after a year,

Everything he had deeply loved,

In his eyes, was gone for good.

I remember the fireplace,

Of which I was especially fond.

This house was meant to be a nice place,

For us to build a family, to bond.

Nothing much of our shared dreams,

Ever came to reality.

But this particular corner of our lost home,

Until this day appeals to me.

So if I ever get to move into a place,

Somewhat like this,

I imagine it will be a small consolation,

To the man I so deeply miss.

34

Part Three: On a Lighter Note

After All, it's not that Bad

Nightmares lose their sense of horror,

As daylight finds its first way in.

When loss if felt to all its extremes,

There's a hope that one might win.

From some sort of emotional bankruptcy,

To some kind of steady growth.

I am learning how to analyse,

In order to understand them both.

I would be so very foolish

To deprive myself from luck.

Depression loses its sense of captivity,

As acceptance finds its first way in.

When loss is felt to all its extremes,

There's no fear of wanting to win.

From this immeasurable damage,

To undefined feelings of affection.

As a human being, I'm a herd animal,

All I needed was a steady connection.

And I am so very foolish,

To feel so wonderstruck.

Step by Step

Step by step you made your way

Your backpack filled with promises

That no one ever kept.

While on the road you faced

The truth of the dark nights

During which you never slept

And all that you could think of

Was the red cross on your map.

Mountain by mountain you were climbing

Your back aching from all the weight

You've been carrying all the way.

While on the road you faced

The truth of the long nights

Never truly becoming day.

And all that you could think of

Was this gaping gap

Representing your deepest desires,

The wishes you'd never spoken out.

Holding the torch with both your hands

Inner voices talking loud

Owning up to the fact that

You never got your right.

It's been like war forever

It never was a productive fight

Until you walked away from her

There's no opponent in an enemy

From whom there's nothing to win

And so you went on to pick your battles

More wisely than before

There's no sense in fighting fire

When there's no forest anymore.

To Give and Take

I try to never ask him,

To do things that he doesn't want to.

And I do not smoke a cigarette,

Before he needs a kiss.

I've learned to be this patient,

I understand the situation.

But is it ever enough?

Tell me, is this love?

There are places you can't go,

Things you might never know.

Cause there is a very thin line.

Between what's ours,

What's yours,

And what's mine.

I am trying to sustain,

This little room I am in.

The more that I fight him,

The more he's breaking in.

But that! That what he's taking,

That piece of me he's breaking,

That was all I had.

Good God, I can't live like that!

There are places I can't go,

Things that I might never show.

There is a very thin line.

Between what's ours,

What's yours,

And what's mine.

Go on and take me, take it all.

But this is my very last call.

Take my body, take my heart,

Take my ending, take my start.

Come to be happy,

Come to be sad.

But stay out of my head.

Young Love

You are the first man

I have ever loved

With no abstention.

With our hearts in sync,

You had my full attention.

Our love was the key

To temper my mind

For a moment

I left all my worries behind.

When we made love

Our bodies were fused

As if we were one

So undivided

And when we were as close

As we could possibly be

I just wanted you

Deeper inside of me.

Then when there was no energy left to release

When our eyes teared up

With this new form of peace

We'd just lay there

With no needs left to be met.

These are the moments

I will never forget.

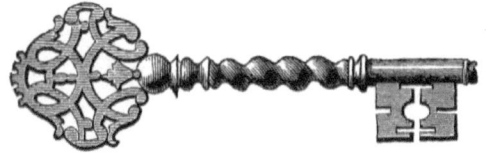

Coping Mechanisms

For some time I have questioned

The moon flaw in my brain.

I have questioned my own abilities,

Am I intelligent?

Am I sane?

Then after a while I noticed,

Everybody has their own kind of way,

To cope with the ongoing challenges,

That come both at night and day.

My dearest, if you're reading this,

You'll be perfectly fine, don't worry.

You're entitled to some strange behaviour,

Don't feel ashamed,

Please don't be sorry.

The ways in which we cope,

With our tension and our fatigue,

Don't just put us on the spot,

They make us profoundly unique.

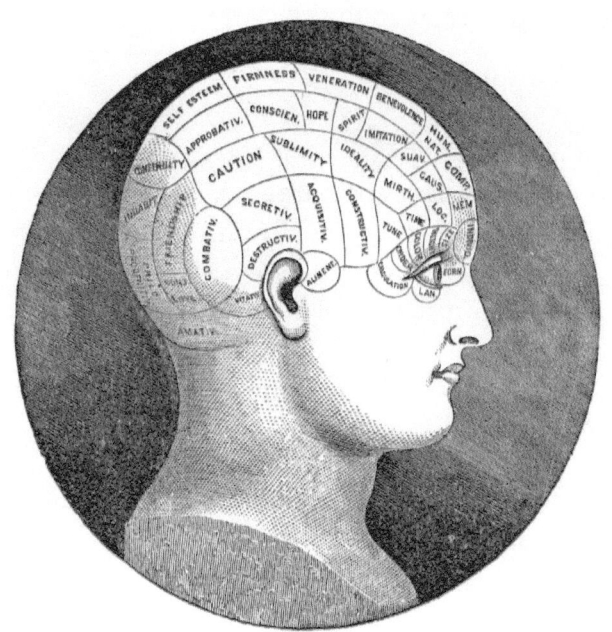

Message in a Bottle

Been standing on the shore
Wondering what life is like
On your side of the sea.
Heard you got access to the
Finest, clearest water
And a giant kitchen garden
Where you grow your apple tree.

My mind wanders to the children,
And what it must be like
To drink in unlimited love,
Do they constantly need
To feed themselves or,
Is it sometimes
Perfectly enough?

I'll write you a message in a bottle,

I don't have your address

Can't mail a postcard straight to your door

You've always been so out of reach,

It's hard to feel the distance

Without wishing to be close

Without feeling I need,

Just a tiny bit more.

My Hands (Part 3)

Restarted life so very tired

As if my battery's unwired

But acceptance is slowing growing

At the bottom of my heart.

Half my brain is shutting down

In my vivid dreams, I drown

In the feelings that I muted

And am now ready to feel.

With my fate

In my own hands.

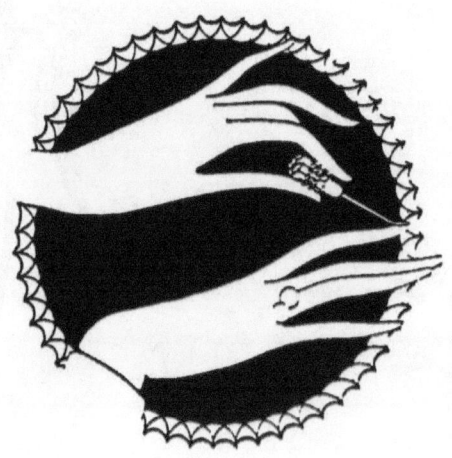

Part Four: For the Record

The Change

I am writing you this letter because I know this

Is the last time that I let our creator create.

Chaos in my life, and that's why I need to go

Somewhere far away for a while,

But I'll be there if you come looking for me,

And I will help you out with anything,

No questions asked.

And then sometimes you might feel like

I abandoned you, but this is not the case

I am just not in a place where I can take

Good care of you -nor myself, without risking

Damaging either one of us and that might

Have permanent consequences

No repetition of the past.

And so I am writing these words, for one day

You might read them and understand why I

Didn't come back after eating pasta and solving

A Rubik's cube together. But I will think of you

Every step of the way. And then when we

Meet again someday, all of us will have grown

And fit right back together.

Because love for your siblings

Is something that will always last.

Let's Start Over

I got many apologies
I still have to make,
Got a record in my head,
Got a long list of mistakes.
And even though it seems
I always get my little way
I really do know,
When I'm not doing okay.

And even though my guilt
Does not always seem to show,
These regrets are like weeds,
Underneath it all, they grow.

I got many debts
I still have to repay,
Got too many truths
I still got to say.

And though it might seem,

I've moved on to forget,

I really do remember,

Sometimes I get upset.

And even though some of my actions,

Were pathetic, so very low.

It's not like I enjoyed them,

I'm aware of what I owe.

If I left anything unanswered,

Come to me, though it's late.

Maybe we can talk things through,

And start with a clean slate.

Seasoned Eyes are Beaming

If you ever live to be eighty

You went through more than

Twenty nine thousand days.

Your timeworn body will

Have changed your

Self-presenting face.

You might have changed

Some of your fundamental convictions

Over your many turbulent years.

You might have developed

And eventually conquered,

Some very deeply rooted fears.

If you ever live to be eighty,

You went through more than

You have grown to imagine today.

With hopefully nothing left to prove

But probably so many meaningful

Words, you'll know just how to say.

You might have drowned in many nightmares,

You might have been absent

While daydreaming.

But when you look back at your

Younger years, your

Seasoned eyes are beaming.

Spirit Animals

Do you know,

You looked just like a snake,

The way you stalked

Your unsuspecting prey.

So silently you watched them graze,

Until you were too close for them to get away.

Like a hyena you would eat the left-over bodies,

You'd pick the already damaged

To avoid the real fight.

The ones who were clearly

Bleeding their heart out,

So there was no way for them to hide.

And as foolish as a city-dove I would be

Drawn to the wrong sources every now and again.

Like some sort of self-destructive woman,

Always looking for the wrong kind of men.

I tried to come as strong as a bear though,
Enough to withstand your sneaky attacks.
But in the end you stripped my soul bare,
Highlighting all the imperfect cracks.

My lack of reality, when it comes to you,
It's like I keep on forgetting the things I should do.
It's like I forget what way I was supposed to take,
It's not easy to come back
From the umpteenth heartbreak.

'Cause yesterday you loved me,
You know, yesterday I was well.
But now I remember it is always,
That hypnotic snake's spell.

So I will run like a leopard,
I'll go as fast as I possibly can.
Like the donkey and the hole,
This won't be happening again.

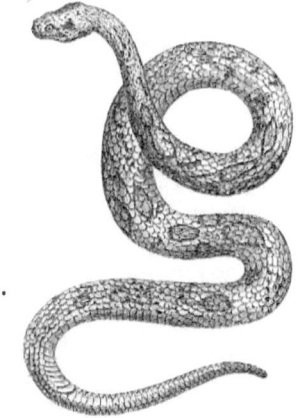

He Loved the Way I Looked

You have this way of looking at me,

The minute you see me, you smile.

These smiles travel a long way,

They stick with me, for quite a while.

You have a way of making me feel beautiful,

Like I'm wrapped in the perfect tone of skin,

I loved being your trophy girl,

But you didn't see what's within.

If anyone ever marries me,

I want him to like my voice.

Not just the way I look by day,

But to appreciate my freedom of choice.

You have this way of looking at me,

And you like to show me off to your friends.

You've always been a man of looks,

Obsessed with buying expensive brands.

This idleness is fun sometimes,

Everyone wants to look their best.

But I mind most what's beyond all that,

I'm here, I'm stripped, undressed.

When the Body Speaks

I know it from the itching of my skin,
The truth keeps forcing its way in.
I want to trust you and your words,
But actions do speak louder.

And I'm not calling you a liar,
But when there's smoke,
Somewhere there must be fire.
The alarm bells - keep on ringing louder.

I know it from the aching of my head,
Something's wrong about what you just said.
I want to trust you and your beautiful blue eyes,
But the spoken contradictions tell me more.

I'm not saying that I knew it all along,
But I do recognize the melody
Of your repetitious song.
And I must admit that I don't like it,
Like I did before.

Every Horse

Every horse thinks its own pack heaviest

But does that mean you're the only one in pain?

You keep telling me about all the ways

You have been wronged in,

I feel that this is driving you insane.

I have been trying to convince you,

You don't have to do this on your own.

From sunset 'till the early morning hours,

I cannot get blood from a stone.

Spent days leading this horse to water,

But there is no way that I could make it drink.

I have tried to tell you

In as many ways as possible,

But none of my words could make you think.

Spider

Somehow you're always in the middle,
Like a spider you control.
You place your traps so secretly,
Into your web, we constantly fall.

You pull the strings so subtly,
Just when one of us tries to escape.
You play with our thoughts and eventually,
We become children who doubt,
Even what our eyes can see.

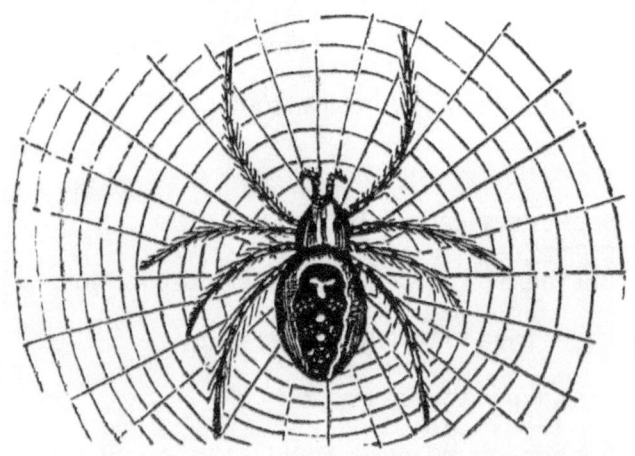

The Sun is my God

The Sun doesn't need any prayers from us,

No commitments, no Bible,

It doesn't need love.

No forgiveness, no prayers, no sins,

The Sun is where all life begins.

The Sun doesn't need any prayers from us,

It will inevitably be our centre above.

Through happiness, grief and despair,

The Sun will always be there.

The Sun doesn't ask perfection from me,

It's a religion that doesn't breed fear.

And even if we'd all stop believing,

The Sun would not disappear.

Part Five: What I wanted to Say Was

My Hands (Part 4)

You've seen my frozen body,

Perfectly still, on one side of the table.

You were wearing your name tag,

And I was wearing my label.

And I couldn't bear for you to look at me,

When my mask was starting to crack.

Doing nothing while I was unravelling,

Was just as hurtful as a ruthless attack.

And so I asked you not to face me,

Whenever I seemed that painfully broken.

-Just to leave the real question unspoken.

I sat on your couch so very tired

As if my battery's unwired

As if nothing you could say,

Would give the courage for me to stay.

And just when I was freezing to death,

I got the one thing I never had,

Pheromones and oxytocin,

Wrapped in a prohibited impulse,

-You gave me back my pulse.

With your hands,

Warming my hands.

All Roads Lead to Rome

I was lost in no one's land,
Gave a finger, then lost my hand.
I went down a road,
I can't begin to explain.

And everybody just seems to know,
Exactly when and where to go.
While I was constantly improvising,
Trying to keep up.

They said there's mother nature,
In everything little thing we see.
I just wish I had a little mother nature,
Naturally, inside of me.

And so I pick flowers on the go,

Knowing exactly when and where they grow.

And while everybody's in line,

I wander freely,

To the same destination.

Growing Comfortable

Talking about the basics of being,

The way we are wired,

The colour we're seeing:

Our most fundamental trust lies with

The ones we know from the heart.

From the point where you start

To mirror each other,

To forgetting to hide your habit to sing.

Like I do when washing my grandma's dishes,

Or when I want to remember a certain thing.

To feel it when someone is vulnerable,

Moved, or still processing what's happening.

To the point where the present

Feels sound enough,

To not think of what tomorrow might bring.

From the depths of our most human melodrama,

To the ends of our most optimistic Futurama,

I think we've always met

Through our mutual tendency

To read between the most significant of lines.

I Prefer Travelling Alone

One bag and a notebook,
Two biscuits and a coffee-to-go.
With every step towards the door,
My courage starts to grow.

For years I have been left to
My own little devices.
All this time I've been trying to
Figure out their costumed disguises.

One bag and a notebook,
Two wishes and one goal.
Leaving the ones I was born with,
Weighed heavily on my soul.

For years I have been left to

Find acceptance of my solitary ways.

All this time I've been forced to,

Work a job that never really pays.

One bag and a notebook,

Two hands and a weakened voice.

I took the road less travelled,

And it got me to live by choice.

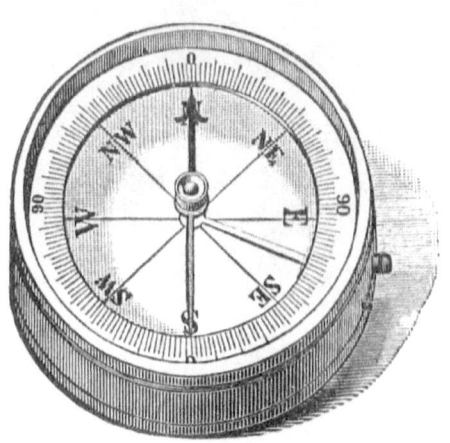

An Imperceptible Being

With the fungi spores I'm hiding,

In the air- just like a virus,

Imperceptible,

But present,

I'll infect you.

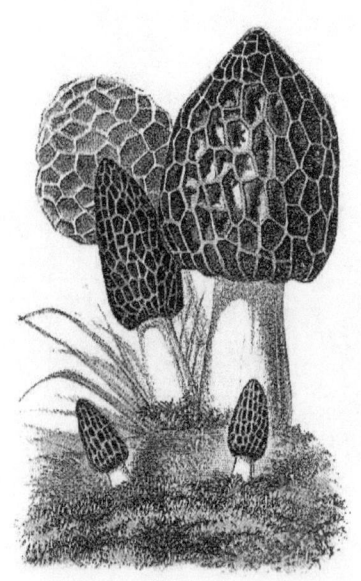

Muhrl's Wisdom

His skin was beautifully brown as chocolate,
But there was ill-looking yellow around his eyes.
He had been asking for spare change,
But failed in most of his tries.

It was an especially cold winter,
And day was about to turn to night.
Why is this kind looking man,
Out in the cold, sleeping outside?

I was taught never to give money,
And so I bought two cups of tea.
After sitting down on a station's bench,
He introduced himself to me.

I asked him if he had some wisdom,
Some words of his own invention.
The homeless man smiled and told me,
"I live with no abstention."

Time Will Pass Anyway

Seconds turn into minutes,

The minutes make the hours.

Time passes by so very slowly,

But these seeds still grow

Into flowers.

At the End

For years I have been dreaming
Of meeting that mythical white light.
However now that death's approaching,
My weary eyes won't close at night.
Because it's always been important
For me to pass in peace.
Always wished for death to be,
That one euphoric release.
Many years of making decisions
Have determined my path like this.
At last I need to allow myself,
To see my life for what it is.
And remember why I let myself,
Hurt the people close to me
To let go of the hidden pain,
That I passed on unknowingly.
For the very first and last time,
I'm returning to the start.
To the place where I once belonged
And might have lost my heart.

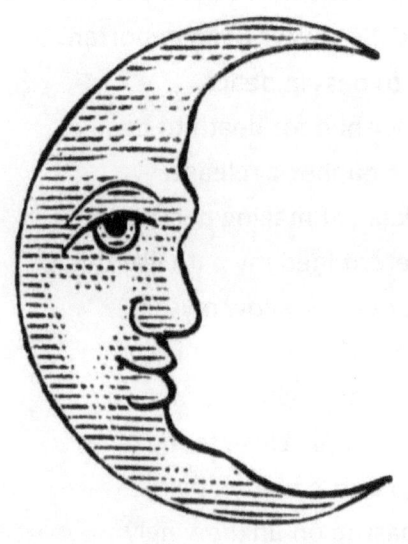